I0164744

Letter 3: What is Global Ethic?

by Leonard Swidler, PhD

About iPubCloud.com

iPubCloud.com is the Digital Publishing arm of iPub Global Connection, LLC. Focusing on globally transformative books from authors all over the world, we value and help promote the works of creators who influence our world in matters of equality, interfaith dialogue, psychology, philosophy, and planet sustainability.

Our value to you is simplicity and convenience. The continually curated book list is culled from the New York Times, Amazon reader reviews and iPub subject matter advisors. You may be confident when you select an item from our store; everything is fulfilled by Amazon, its affiliates, and other important distribution channels.

There are many books like this one on iPubCloud.com along with selections of other categories of books. Don't keep us a secret. Connect with us on Facebook and join our mailing list. And, if you have a story to tell, reach out.

iPub Global Connection, LLC
https://www.iPubCloud.com
550 W. Baseline Rd., #303
Mesa, AZ 85210
info@iPubCloud.com

Contents

Introduction

"Will" is short for Willow Athena Swidler-Notte, my fantastic grand-daughter, born at the beginning of the Third Millennium (2000), to whose house I have been going practically every weekend since 2011, to teach her German (which is why I am addressed as *Opa*, a typical German abbreviation for Grandpa), and slowly talk about all kinds of interesting things in life—and end up having a vegetarian dinner with Will and my brilliant daughter Eva and her wonderful husband Ian (both are professors, Ian high school ecology/biology, and Eva university history).

These are my letters to Will, with whom—when you meet her, you will understand why—I clearly am madly in love.

Opa,

Len Swidler, (*info@ipubcloud.com*)

Letter No. 3: A Global Ethic?

Dear Will,

I am glad you picked up on the idea of a "Global Ethic" that I wrote about at the end of my last letter, the one on how we know what is right and what is wrong. You obviously have a sense for important ideas. You know, Will, it is interesting that the "idea" of a Global Ethic—at least as it is talked about these days—is new, but the "reality" of a Global Ethic really goes back long before we even invented writing. I know that you remember that the Sumerians first invented writing around 2500 B.C.E.

OK, Will, I also know you have been studying Egyptian hieroglyphics and therefore realize that the Egyptians can also make a case that they too were involved with the development of writing. However, you also know that their writing system did not spread beyond Egypt, whereas the Sumerian cuneiform manner of writing quickly spread all over the Mesopotamian region. You remember seeing those really ancient Sumerian cuneiform clay tablets in the University of Pennsylvania Archeology Museum.

1. Articulation of Ethics—In Laws

You also read about the stone *style* (or pillar) from the eighteenth century B.C.E. with the laws of Hammurabi chiseled on it; and everybody in America knows about the Ten Commandments said to have been given to Moses on Mount Sinai, perhaps in the fourteenth century B.C.E. Of course, you also know, Will, that often scholars disagree about dating ancient documents and events.

In any case, various rules of right and wrong are very old and very widespread all over the world. Hence, for thousands of years, practically all human beings agreed on some of the most important ideas of right and wrong. So, yes, Will, you can go back and study ancient history and learn that there was a kind of "Global Ethic" already four thousand years ago if not even much earlier. We find that basically, everybody thought that killing innocent persons was wrong, that lying, stealing... were all wrong.

2. Beginning Awareness of a Global Ethic

Yet, there is something new about the talk about a Global Ethic today, Will. First of all, until relatively recently, hardly anybody knew how to read. You might be thinking, so what difference does that make? That means that very few people knew about civilization and society beyond their next-door neighbors. Remember, until the Industrial Revolution (started in England only in the late eighteenth century), practically everybody (90+%) made their living by farming and were illiterate. They probably never traveled more than a day or two's walk from home in their lifetime. So, they knew only their closest friends and the occasional passerby, like a trader or the like. Some of those traveling peddlers, of course, were serious people, but many of them were the equivalent of "snake oil" sellers. Naturally, most people were probably susceptible to the facts shared with them by outsiders.

The point I am trying to make here, Will, is that most people had no reason to think that other people shared their basic ethical principles. Basically, they didn't even think about other people at all for the most part. Whenever they did think about other people, it was because something forced them to think about them. Perhaps they were being invaded by another nation, or perhaps they only heard about others being invaded. Often, the wildest things tended to be said about the "Other"—and nothing could gainsay it, for 90+% of the population did not travel anywhere, nor could they read! So, you see, Will, the vast majority of people either knew nothing about different people or most often held very untrue, weird ideas about them and their customs.

It is only in modern times that significant numbers of people begin to learn about the ways and thoughts of other cultures or ethnic groups. As you know, public education didn't even get started until well into the nineteenth century, and then only in certain parts of the West. Remember, Will, when my Dad—your great grandfather—was born in 1897, not only was there no worldwide internet, there were no movies, no television, nor was there radio! There were no rockets to the moon and planets, there were no airplanes, and the vast majority of people still traveled by horse and buggy. So, Will, you are very, very different from all the human beings who lived 200,000 years before you. You, and now hundreds of millions of other humans know increasingly more and more about other people, about how they live and think.

More than that, these millions of others are not only knowable by you and others like you, they are so much "in your face," that the question of what we have—or don't have—in common simply asks itself! We can hardly avoid asking the question, Will!

You, of course, have heard and read much about negative attitudes like racism, Antisemitism, Islamophobia—in other words, hatred of other races, hatred of Jews, hatred of Muslims. Most of that hatred is based on ignorance. Most people in the past and still many people today grow up in more or less traditional communities, each of

10

which says to its members, "This is the right way to understand the world and how to act in it—if we did not think it was the correct way (automatically implying that all other ways are simply mistaken) we wouldn't be teaching it to you!"

However, Will, you and your generation are in a radically different situation from all other people born before you! As I pointed out before, "Everybody" is sitting in your own living room! They all sneak in through the radio, the television, through what we read, and now through all the connecting paths of the Internet (remember, the Internet was invented by Tim Berners Lee only in 1989—just a few years before you were born!). This massive fact has a massive impact—both negative and positive. Let's talk about those two impacts.

3. Clash of Civilizations

First the negative impact. Will, you have probably never heard of a Harvard scholar named Samuel P. Huntington. He wrote first an article (in 1992) and then a book arguing that after the Cold War (when the world was divided in two after the Second World War, between the supporters of world Communism and the supporters of the "Free" World), the world fell into a "Clash of Civilizations." Huntington listed several Civilizations: Western, Orthodox, Islamic, African, Hindu, Buddhist, Sinic, and Japanese.

Well, Will, one could argue about the listing of these eight so-called separate civilizations, but surely it is clear that there are a number of very different ways of "Understanding the ultimate meaning of life, and how to live accordingly"— which is basically what we mean when we talk about "religions," or their secular equivalents. As we noted above, even in your great-grandfather's day most people in the world were only vaguely aware of those "Others." 90+% of the world really didn't know about the "Other." Then, quite suddenly, the Other came crashing into our everyday life. Our first reaction—and it is still going on, especially with those don't have very wide experiences or reading—is fear and hatred! That, Will, obviously leads to what Huntington called the "Clash of Civilizations"!

Unfortunately, this fear and hatred of the Other— and the potential violence—is something that will only grow when there is a major physical movement of peoples. This became very visible in 2017 in Europe when millions of refugees flooded into Europe from the war-torn Middle East and poverty-stricken Africa.

Tragically, as you are well aware, Will, it became even more visible in the United States with the election of Donald Trump. All those millions of Americans who, for a wide variety of reasons, harbored resentments against the "Other" began to feel permitted, even encouraged, to act out—to give voice to their insecurity, resentment, and even naked hatred. This period will doubtlessly become even more intense. In fact, it is your age cohort, Will, which will take the lead in turning America, and thereby the rest of the world, away from this backward-looking last-gasp "tribalist" attitude to embrace and live with an ever-expanding Global Ethic.

4. Dialogue of Civilizations

Now, that is a glimpse at the negative side of the so-called "Clash of Civilizations." As you know by now, every plus in life has a minus, every up has a down, every light has a dark, and so on. There is also very much a positive side, which many obviously call the *"Dialogue* of Civilizations." In fact, Will, I have recently written a book with the title, *The Age of Global Dialogue*[1] which, as the title suggests, argues that even more characteristic than the *Clash* is the *Dialogue* among civilizations.

On the positive side: The very fact of being forced into each other's living rooms has led not only to the initial fear but now more and more to the mature move of asking questions about the Other—and then, inevitably, about our own Selves! Will, asking questions is the opening and continuing move of Dialogue. We increasingly want to know more about how the Other thinks and acts. One of the big "wins" in this questioning is that we

[1] Leonard Swidler, *The Age of Global Dialogue* (Eugene, OR: Wipf and Stock, 2016).

come to know more interesting things about the Other—and, perhaps even more interestingly, we come to know more about ourselves! We begin to investigate what and how we think and act—often unconsciously, unthinkingly—and wow (!) we begin to learn that there are many things we thought and did—without really even knowing why.

One of the things we begin to learn about the Other is that we, in fact, have many things held in common. It is very often in the area of "right and wrong" that we find we hold many principles in common. They compose what my friend Hans Küng and I, starting in the early 1990s, called the *Global Ethic*—those basic ethical principles that the vast majority of human beings around the world, in fact, hold in common.

5. The Content of the Global Ethic

OK, OK, Will, I can hear you in my mind asking about what some of these basic ethical principles are! All right, let's get to at least some of them by asking ourselves some simple questions. We have already reached agreement on the Golden Rule, which practically every ethical and religious system has spelled out, starting with Zoroaster, Confucius, Buddha, and the Torah (Hebrew Bible) already in the fifth century B.C.E.

Speaking of the Torah immediately suggests that we take a look at the so-called Ten Commandments, which according to the book of Exodus in the Old Testament (Torah) were given to Moses on Mount Sinai. Embedded in those Ten Commandments are several other notions that we also find turning up across the board in all kinds of human communities.

Think about it, Will: which of those Ten would you say everybody agrees with? How about Commandment Eight, the one that says, "Thou shall not lie"? Hmm. Well, what if everybody assumed that it was all right to lie? What do you think would happen to everyday life?

I can just hear you thinking, Wow! It would be total chaos! Nobody could do anything with anybody else, because you wouldn't be able to trust what anyone said they did or will do. To be sure that something was done, you would have to do everything yourself! Well, then things could never improve because you couldn't even bank on your own husband or wife or children doing what they said they would, let alone other folks! Human life would simply collapse!

Remember, Will, in an earlier Letter, we figured out that the very purpose of "speaking" is to communicate a thought in my mind to your mind —hence, communicating something different than what is in my mind upends the very purpose of talking, of words, and therefore, we decided that lying is fundamentally bad. Remember, in our earlier discussion about what we mean when we say something is "good," we saw that it has to do with how we understand the purpose of that thing; concerning "talking," its purpose is to communicate what is in my mind to someone else's mind.

So, we can say that lying is bad both in itself—that is, it is contrary to the very purpose of speaking— and, further, we can also say that widespread lying would be totally destructive to society!

Therefore, Will, those two reasons alone dictate that every human community which has continued to exist more than a couple of generations *had to* have ethical rules against lying—otherwise they wouldn't exist today. They all would've self-destructed!

All right, now we are making progress! Let's now try a more demanding commandment: "Thou shall not steal." Again, Will, let's ask ourselves, what if it was OK for everybody to just take what someone else had made or earned? Again, Will, I can just hear you thinking, Wow! In that case, everybody would be stealing from everybody else—only the strongest would get everything! Of course, that wouldn't work very well, because then nobody would bother to make anything; a stronger guy would just come along and steal it. Of course, Will, you no doubt are thinking that a smart guy would figure out ways to hide his things so they couldn't be stolen. But that would keep us all at a pretty primitive level. How are you going to hide a house that you build for yourself!?

Nah, you are thinking, just like with lying, if stealing was OK, it would produce a society which was pretty limited. We would never possess more than the absolute minimum—and that would all be eaten away by non-productive strongmen. Again, such a society would probably not exist beyond a couple of generations. So, Will, once again, I am sure that you would want to say that— regardless of the rightness/wrongness of stealing in itself, no society could exist if it did not have ethical rules against stealing.

Will, I think that we can see a pattern developing here. What we have argued about (concerning lying and stealing) applies, even more, when it comes to murder! (Commandment Five: "Thou shall not kill.") What would happen to a society if it was OK to kill anybody you felt like killing!? Poof! It wouldn't last even a generation! And then, what of the Sixth Commandment: "Thou shall not commit adultery!" This commandment, in a way, blends Commandments eight (not lying, being honest) and seven (not stealing), and folds them into a long-term intimate relationship between a man and a woman. A public commitment is made not to betray your partner (Eighth Commandment) and not to prey upon another's (Seventh Commandment).

OK, Will, I hear you loud and clear! You are saying that these commitments, as well as practically all other so-called ethical rules about male-female relations, have been, and still are bent toward unjustly favoring the male. You are totally right, Will!

But! That has been changing for many decades now. Just think, Will, over a century and a half ago (when we Americans fought our bloody Civil War), most established religions and ethical systems still thought slavery was ethically acceptable, as it had been for thousands (!) of years. Today it is totally gone! Sure, various kinds of slavery still persist in parts of the world—but no public thinker or public leader would claim today it is ethically acceptable. It is gone!

Well, Will, that is why, if you look at the three drafts of a Global Ethic that have already been drafted, you will see that the equality of women with men is already included:

http://dialogueinstitute.org/global-ethic-documents/.

Why don't you look over at your leisure the documents about a Global Ethic at that website? Then, we could further talk about what those shared ethical principles—that *Global Ethic*—are in some detail, if you wish. Then we should at least eventually also talk about the many "differences" that we encounter in the Other.

In the meanwhile, I look forward, Will, to your reflections and questions about what we have discussed here.

Liebe,

Opa

Do Not Miss Out

Other Books in the Series

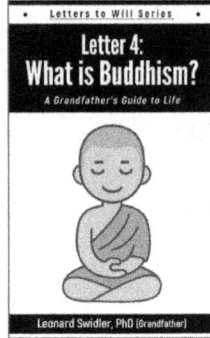

www.ingramcontent.com/pod-product-compliance
Lightning Source LLC
Chambersburg PA
CBHW060550030426
42337CB00021B/4522